Somehow it's all connected.
The chain spins the sprocket.
And a gear makes it go.
This machine is a marvel!

Bike Shop

Does your bicycle need fixing? You may want to bring it to a nearby bike shop. The shop is a busy place. Many people bring in their bicycles to be fixed. As you wait your turn, you notice workers pushing and pulling different objects. One worker is pulling on a wrench, tightening a nut. Another worker is pushing the pedals of a bike backward, oiling the chain.

A worker tells you that your bike will be easy to fix. A few bolts have to be tightened, and you will be ready to ride. You don't need a new bicycle. The owner lets you borrow one for a test ride anyway.

- What objects have you pushed or pulled today?

- What tools do you think are needed to fix a flat tire?

- Which machines would you miss if they were broken or missing?

FORCES & MACHINES

BIKE
SHOP

Chapter 1

Force and Work   6–23

Forces   10–15
Work   16–19

Chapter 2

Simple Machines   24–45

Levers   28–33
Inclined Planes   34–37
Machines with Wheels   38–41

Chapter 3

Compound Machines 46–59

Putting Simple
  Machines Together   50–53
Compound Machines
  Are Everywhere   54–57

Activities

How do forces affect objects?	8–9
How can you decrease friction?	14
How can you do work?	18
Are all lotions and oils the same?	21
Why do things slide?	23
Are you using a machine?	26–27
How can a simple machine make your work easier?	29
Can you use an inclined plane?	35
Can you pull together?	39
When should you use a simple machine?	45
How can you design a gadget?	48–49
Can you find compound machines?	50
Where does the force go?	52
What is in a compound machine?	59

Features

Side Trip: The Tumbling Show	13
Viewpoint: Cycling	20
Science, Technology & Society: Arthritis	33
Science & Literature Connection	42–43
Dilemma: How Ramps Are Added to Buildings	55
Career Corner: Rehabilitation Engineer	57

Chapter 1

Force and Work

Have you ever thought about all the pushes and pulls that take place while you are riding a bike? You push the pedals. The chain pulls toothed wheels called sprockets. The tires push against the road as the bicycle moves. The air and the bicycle push against each other. If you go fast, you feel the air push against you, too. Look at the picture of the bike handlebars on this page. What causes the streamers on the ends of the handles to flutter?

As you pedal your bike up a hill you may notice that your legs have to force the pedals down harder. And when you go down a hill, you may not have to pedal at all. What do you think the word *force* means?

Study the words and pictures on these pages for clues about force. How is the boy on the bike on the next page using force? Then write a meaning of force in your Science Journal.

90 ★ Montana
Helena   Billings ● 94 Yellowstor
South Dakota
Columb
Orego
ament
Fresn
5
Los
annel
lands

Explore Activity

How do forces affect objects?

HANDS-ON ACTIVITY

Process Skills

Observing, Inferring

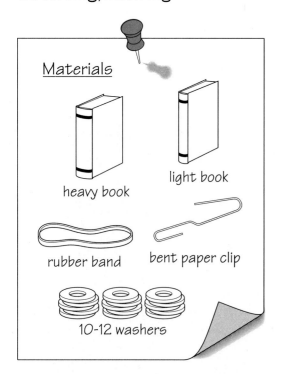

Materials

heavy book

light book

rubber band

bent paper clip

10-12 washers

Observe and Collect Data

1. **ACTIVITY JOURNAL** Stand with your arms held out to the side. Count to 30. Let down your arms. In your Activity Journal, record how your arms felt.

2. Holding one book in each hand, raise your arms to the side again. Keep your arms raised until you count to 30. Lower your arms and put down the books. Record how your arms felt after you put down the books.

3. Loop the rubber band on the end of your finger. Hang the bent paper clip on the rubber band.

4. Add washers one at a time to the hook. **Predict** what will happen to the rubber band as you add the washers. In your Activity Journal, record your observations.

Share Your Results

Compare your results from step 4 with those of two other students. How did their results compare with yours?

Draw Conclusions

1. How did your arms feel after step 1? Did one arm feel more tired than the other arm?
2. How did your arms feel after step 2? Did one arm feel more tired than the other arm? Explain your answer.
3. How did adding washers to the hook change the rubber band?

Apply What You Know

1. How would your arms have felt if you had held two books in each hand? Explain.
2. Why did fifteen washers have a greater effect on the rubber band than one?

Texas · 45 · Louisiana · Gulf of Mexico

What are the different kinds of forces?

A **force** is a push or pull. A force can act on an object to change its motion. When you toss a ball into the air, you use a force to push it upward. Another force pulls the ball back down. Why do you think that happens?

A force can start an object moving or make it move faster. A bicycle moves forward when you push down on the pedals.

A force can change the direction in which an object is moving. When you turn the handle-bars on a moving bike you are changing the direction of the bike's force.

A force can make an object change shape. A bicycle tire changes shape when you fill the tube inside it with air. The air pushes outward against the tube, which pushes against the tire.

A force can slow or stop an object that is moving. The younger child is trying to push down the pedals of the tricycle to move away. The older child is pulling back on the moving bike. The older child can slow and even stop the younger child's bike from moving.

The riders in this race are using force to move their bicycles. As the muscles in a rider's legs push down on the bike's pedals, the bike moves forward. How can the racers make their bikes go faster?

What is gravity?

Have you ever heard someone say, "What goes up must come down"? This is a statement about a force called gravity. **Gravity** is a pulling force between one object and another. Gravity pulls a falling baseball toward the ground. It holds cyclists on bicycle seats and students at desks. It holds the earth in its orbit around the sun. Look at the picture of the children on this page. Why does their hair hang this way when they are upside down?

SCIENCE JOURNAL Measure the force of gravity between you and the earth. It's easy. Just step on the bathroom scale. In your Science Journal, write how much you weigh. Now hold something heavy in your hands and weigh yourself again. How did holding something heavy affect the force between you and the earth?

BACK HOME

The Tumbling Show

It's always fun to watch the Jesse White tumblers perform. They have been on television and perform more than 750 times a year. They perform all across the country.

Notice how the tumbler seems to fly across the floor. No matter how high he jumps, he always comes back to the earth. What is the force that brings him back down?

Amazing!

You would weigh almost three times as much on Jupiter as you weigh on Earth.

What is friction?

Could you safely ride a bicycle on a sidewalk? Yes, you could. Could you safely ride a bike on a frozen pond? No! The bike would slip on the ice. There would not be enough friction between the bike tires and the ice.

Friction is a force that slows or stops moving objects. Friction occurs when objects rub against each other. It is common for objects to rub together.

It happens whenever you ride your bicycle. What objects rub together when you ride a bike?

In machines, friction slows moving parts and makes them wear out. One way to decrease friction and let things slide a bit is to put oil on the objects that rub together. Oil is put on bike chains to lessen friction between the chain and sprockets.

Be a Scientist

HANDS-ON ACTIVITY

How can you decrease friction?

1. ACTIVITY JOURNAL Put the palms of your hands together. Quickly rub your hands back and forth for about 15 or 20 seconds. How do your palms feel now? In your Activity Journal, write how your palms feel.

2. Repeat the experiment with lotion or oil on your palms.

Predict what you think will happen now. How will your palms feel after rubbing them together this time? Explain in your Activity Journal how your hands feel. What would happen if you repeated this experiment using water on your palms?

Tires come in many widths and tread patterns. Tires for a dirt bike are wide and have deep treads. These tires cause more friction than other tires. Bikes with these tires are safer to ride on loose dirt.

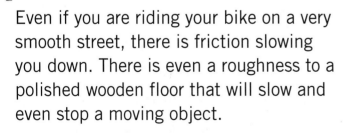

Even if you are riding your bike on a very smooth street, there is friction slowing you down. There is even a roughness to a polished wooden floor that will slow and even stop a moving object.

How are you doing?

1. Name two kinds of forces.
2. You jump off a diving board into a pool. Describe the force that sends you into the air. Name the force that slows your motion.
3. Think Why are the soles of sneakers different from other shoes?

The bike shop worker is lifting a bike onto a rack to fix it. When he lifts an object, he is doing work.

What is work?

You do many kinds of work every day. You do schoolwork and homework. Sometimes you may help take care of your younger brothers and sisters. Perhaps you make your bed in the morning. Maybe you help wash dishes or clear the table. What are some kinds of work that you do every day?

In science, **work** means something different than it means in everyday life. In science, work is done when a force makes an object move. If an object moves in the direction that you push or pull it, you have done work. Think again about the kinds of work that you said you do each day. Do you use forces to do these things? Would a scientist call these things work? In this lesson we will be using the scientific meaning of the word work.

 In your Science Journal, use a pencil or crayon to draw a line across the page. Did you push the pencil or crayon? Did you do work? Write the meaning of work in everyday life. Then write the meaning of work as you think a scientist might.

Machines, such as bicycles and automobiles, help people do work. Ride a bike when you can. Let the bike help you do the work, rather than a car. You can help limit air pollution and save gasoline.

When you push on something, and it moves in the direction you push it, you are doing work.

SCIENCE JOURNAL Observe a person in your household preparing a meal. In your Science Journal, make a list of everything that the person does in five minutes. Pretend you are a scientist. Put a check next to each item on your list that is scientific work.

BACK HOME

When is work done?

To do work you must use a force to make an object move. When you push or pull an object, you are using force. How much work you do depends on two things—how hard you push or pull and how far the object moves.

These children are doing work. They are pushing and pulling soil to create a garden in their neighborhood.

Be a Scientist

How can you do work?

1. Place four books on the floor. Lift one book onto a chair. Then lift three books onto a chair.
2. 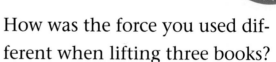 In your Activity Journal, draw a picture showing what you did. Use arrows to show where the lifting force was used.

How was the force you used different when lifting three books?
3. Lift one book onto a chair. Then lift one book onto a high shelf. Draw another picture to show your lifting forces. How were the forces that you used different? How were they the same?

To do work on an object, a force must move the object in the same direction as the force. Which picture shows work being done?

If the object doesn't move, no work is done, no matter how hard you push or pull.

How are you doing?

1. Draw a picture that shows an example of scientific work.
2. Compare work done in everyday life with your example from question 1.
3. Think A girl pushes against a wall. A boy brushes lint from his sweater. Who did more work? Explain.

Cycling

Riding a bike is good exercise. You use your muscles and can observe the world closely as it whizzes past you. Cycling can be fun.

Riding a bike can also be good for the air around you. There probably have been days when the air seemed polluted. That dirty air is caused by cars. If you ride your bike somewhere instead of riding in a car you are helping to keep the pollution out of your air.

In many cities people ride their bikes because it is the best and sometimes only way to get around. Some cities are crowded and bicycles fit more easily on the streets than cars or buses. People need their bikes to get to work or to school. The people in these pictures are using their bikes to get where they need to go. Imagine all of these people in cars instead of on bikes. That would probably be a huge traffic jam!

Are all lotions and oils the same?

Observe and Collect Data

1. Place a small sample of lotion on a piece of wax paper.

2. Write the name of your sample in your Activity Journal. Rub a small bit of the lotion onto the back of your hand. In your journal, note how it feels.

3. Sprinkle a bit of water onto the part of your skin where you put the lotion. Does the water stay in little drops?

4. Repeat steps 1, 2, and 3 with all the samples and record what happens.

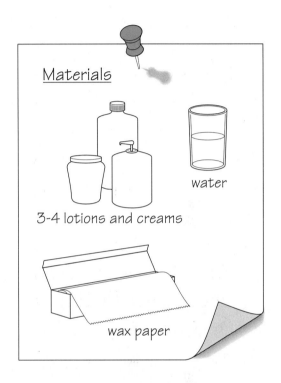

Materials

water

3-4 lotions and creams

wax paper

Draw Conclusions

1. Some lotions soak into the skin quickly, and some do not. What do you think might happen to your bicycle chain if all the oil you used soaked into the metal?

2. Some lotions keep water from soaking into the skin, and some do not. What would happen to your bike chain if the oil you used let water reach the metal?

Looking Back

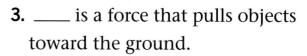

Words and Concepts

Complete the following statements.

1. A push and a pull are words used to describe a(n) ____.
2. A force that slows or stops an object is called ____.

3. ____ is a force that pulls objects toward the ground.
4. To do ____ means to use force to move an object.
5. ____ keeps a bike tire from slipping on a road.
6. Work is done on an object when it is moved in the direction of a ____ applied to it.

Applied Thinking Skills

Answer the following questions. You can use words, drawings, and diagrams in your answers.

7. Why do people spread sand on an icy sidewalk?
8. Describe the forces you must overcome to lift a box off the floor.
9. Look at the picture of the girl lifting some boxes. Draw a picture of her doing less work.
10. **Your World** You let go of a pencil. The pencil falls to the floor. Did you force the pencil to the floor? If you didn't, what did?

Show What You Know

Why do things slide?

Observe and Collect Data

1. Cut a piece of sandpaper to fit one side of a wooden block. Glue it to that side.
2. Place the uncovered block on the board.
3. **Predict** what will happen if you lift one end of the board. Lift the board until the block begins to slide. Measure the height of the upper end of the board. Record the height of the board in your Activity Journal.
4. Repeat step 3 with the sandpaper side of the block facing down.

Draw Conclusions

1. What happened to the block?
2. Compare what happened in steps 3 and 4 above. Which block and ramp was lifted higher before the block began to slide?

Process Skills
Observing, Inferring

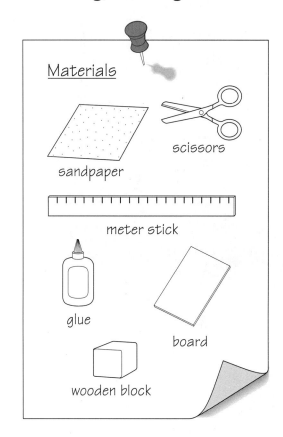

Materials

sandpaper

scissors

meter stick

glue

board

wooden block

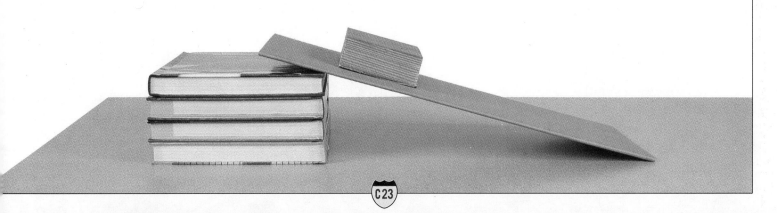

Chapter 2

Simple Machines

You have a flat tire on your bike. You know just how it happened. You found a sharp nail sticking into the tire.

SCIENCE JOURNAL Describe in your Science Journal how a nail could get stuck in your tire. What made the tire go flat?

You do not know how to fix a flat tire, so you take your bike to the bicycle shop. Look at the tools and bike parts you can find at a bike shop. Tools are simple kinds of machines. They can help you do the work of fixing a flat tire.

Suppose you had to use your bare hands to remove the tire from the wheel. Could you do it? A machine known as a tire iron will help you remove the tire and inner tube from the rim. The inner tube can be fixed using a patch kit and put back on your bike.

Suppose you had to use your breath to pump up the mended inner tube. Could you blow up the tube? You probably couldn't blow much air into an inner tube. You can use a bicycle pump to push air into the inner tube. Now your tire is mended and full of air. You're ready to ride your bike again!

Are you using a machine?

Process Skills

Observing, Inferring

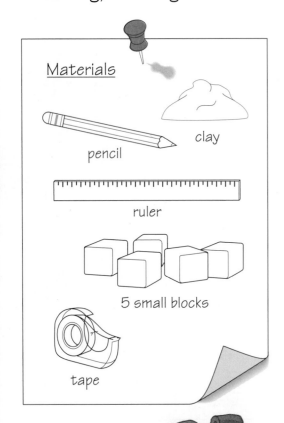

Materials

pencil

clay

ruler

5 small blocks

tape

Observe and Collect Data

1. Use some clay to hold a pencil in place on your desk. Place a ruler on the pencil so that the middle of the ruler is on the pencil.

2. Stack five blocks on one end of the ruler. Add bits of clay to the other end of the ruler until the blocks are lifted and the ruler balances. If the blocks slip off the ruler, use tape to hold them in place.

3. **ACTIVITY JOURNAL** In your Activity Journal, draw the balanced ruler, blocks, and lumps of clay.

4. Take the clay off the end of the ruler and set it aside. Move the pencil so it is now closer to the blocks. Add new clay to the other end of the ruler until the blocks are lifted.

5. In your Activity Journal, draw the balanced ruler, blocks, and clay.

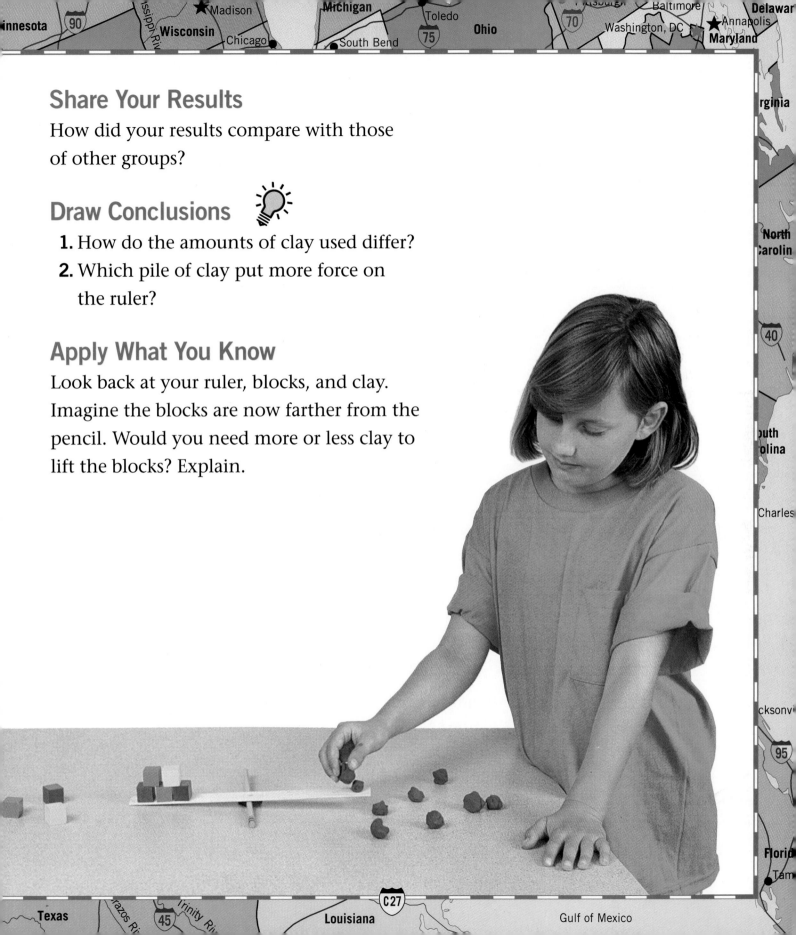

Share Your Results

How did your results compare with those of other groups?

Draw Conclusions

1. How do the amounts of clay used differ?
2. Which pile of clay put more force on the ruler?

Apply What You Know

Look back at your ruler, blocks, and clay. Imagine the blocks are now farther from the pencil. Would you need more or less clay to lift the blocks? Explain.

This boy is sweeping the cement in front of his house. He is using the broom as a lever. His upper hand is the fulcrum. And he is using force with his lower hand to move the broom along the cement. Where is the lever arm? What part of the broom uses friction?

What is a lever?

The ruler and pencil that you used in the activity on pages C26 and C27 worked together as a simple machine. A **simple machine** is something that helps people use forces to make their work easier.

A ruler and pencil can make a lever. A **lever** is a simple machine made up of a stiff arm, or arms, that pivots or turns. The point that a lever turns on is called the **fulcrum** (ful'krem). What part of the ruler-and-pencil lever is the fulcrum? What part is the stiff arm, or lever arm?

You could probably lift the five blocks from the Explore Activity without using a lever. Imagine that each block was a huge, heavy boulder. How do you think a lever could be used to move the boulders?

Be a Scientist

How can a simple machine make your work easier?

1.  Hold the handle of a hammer near the head. Carefully pound a nail into a wooden board.

2. Now hold the handle of the hammer at the end. Pound a second nail into the board, hitting the nail three times. The hammer is a lever. By moving your hand, you changed the length of the lever arm. Which way did the hammer give you more force? How do you know?

3. Use the claw part of the hammer to remove the nails. Used this way, the hammer is another type of lever.

What are some uses of levers?

fulcrum

Levers can be used in many different ways. A nail puller is a type of lever used to remove nails from wood. It is used in the same way a tire iron is used to pry a tire from the rim of a wheel.

The pictures on these pages show different ways levers can be used, from picking up an ear of corn to removing a cap from a soda bottle.

A simple machine is used every time you open a capped bottle of soda. The lever makes it easier to remove the cap.

YOU CAN HELP

Sometimes you create trash, such as a bent nail or an empty soda can, when using simple machines. Recycle that trash properly.

The lever is one of the most common simple machines around. The bottle opener on page C30, a common lever, has been used by people for many years. People learned that they could store things to drink in bottles and cans. And the opener could be used to open the bottles and cans to remove the drinks. How do you think the opener on page C30 could be used to open cans?

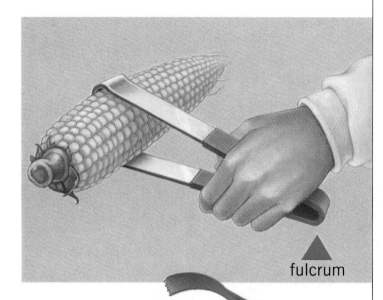
fulcrum

Tongs are a kind of lever that can be used to pick up salad or corn. Where is the force applied on this kind of lever?

 SCIENCE JOURNAL
As you probably remember, a lever has a fulcrum and lever arm. Levers are found in many places. Look around your school or home for levers. List in your Science Journal what levers you have found.

BACK HOME

How are arms and legs like levers?

You have seen that levers help people use forces to make work easier. By placing the fulcrum at different places, levers are used in many ways.

Some bones in your body work together like levers. The places where two bones meet are called joints.

Some of the joints in your body are like fulcrums. The bones on each side of a joint are like lever arms. The drawings below show how parts of your arm and leg are like levers. Can you think of any other joints in your body that are like fulcrums?

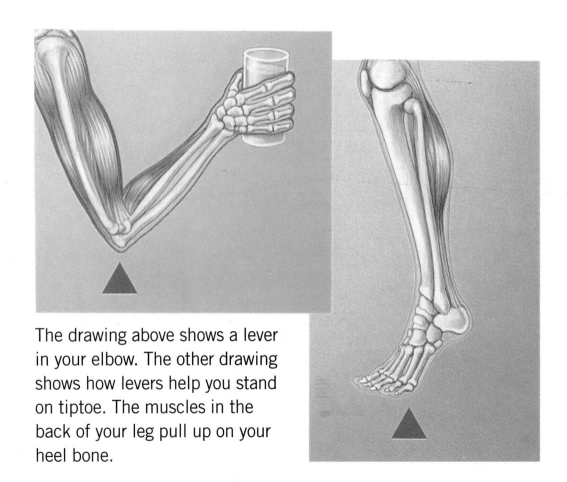

The drawing above shows a lever in your elbow. The other drawing shows how levers help you stand on tiptoe. The muscles in the back of your leg pull up on your heel bone.

Arthritis

Arthritis is a disease that causes joints to swell. Usually older people get arthritis, but many young people also have the condition, or disease. Moving swollen joints can be very painful. So movement is slow and limited. For example, people with arthritis in their hands have trouble picking things up and holding them.

The tools you see on this page are often used by people with arthritis in their arms and hands.

The blue object you see is attached to a key that might open a door or start a car. If you have arthritis in your fingers this would be easier to pick up and grip. The red object can be used to remove lids from bottles or jars.

The long object you see has a comb attached. How do you think this might be used? These and other tools can help people who have arthritis.

How are you doing?

1. Name the parts of a lever.
2. Explain how a simple machine can be helpful.
3. **Think** You observe that a fishing rod is a kind of lever. Draw and label a fishing rod to explain your observation.

What is an inclined plane?

Imagine trying to lift a heavy object, like a motorcycle, straight up onto a truck. With help, you could probably do it, but it would take a lot of force. It would be much easier to roll the motorcycle up a ramp onto the truck. A ramp is an **inclined plane,** a kind of simple machine with a slanted surface. Inclined planes help people raise objects without lifting them straight up.

Look at the boy using a wheelchair on this page. Do you think it is easier for him to go straight up a curb or up an inclined plane? As you may have noticed he could not go up the curb without someone helping him. With a ramp attached to a curb, the boy can either go up or down the curb easily.

Here you see cyclists pedaling up a steep winding road. The road is an inclined plane. The cyclists use less force going up the inclined plane than they would pedaling straight up the side of a hill. They do travel a greater distance to reach the top of the hill. So they don't do less work. The ramp just makes their work easier.

Be a Scientist

Can you use an inclined plane?

1. Attach a rubber band to the front of a roller skate or skateboard. Use the rubber band to slowly lift a skate or skateboard from the floor to a chair seat. Observe how far the rubber band stretches. This shows how much force is used.

2. Use a board to make a ramp to the chair seat. Use the rubber band to pull the skate slowly up the ramp to the chair seat. Note how far the rubber band stretches this time.

3. **ACTIVITY JOURNAL** In your Activity Journal, make two drawings. Show how much the rubber band stretches without using the ramp and with the ramp.

What are screws and wedges?

People use inclined planes to raise objects, including themselves, more easily. A **screw** is an inclined plane wrapped around a post. The ridges of the screw are the inclined plane. The ridges start at the bottom of the post. They wrap around the post many times until they reach the head of the screw. When you drive a screw into wood, the wood moves up the inclined plane. Ridges on drills and bolts are other examples of screws.

A **wedge** is two inclined planes joined back-to-back. Wedges are movable and are used to split objects or to force them apart. The sharp edge of a knife and the head of an axe are two examples of wedges.

As the bolt is turned, the metal of the bicycle reflector moves along the inclined plane formed by the ridges of the bolt.

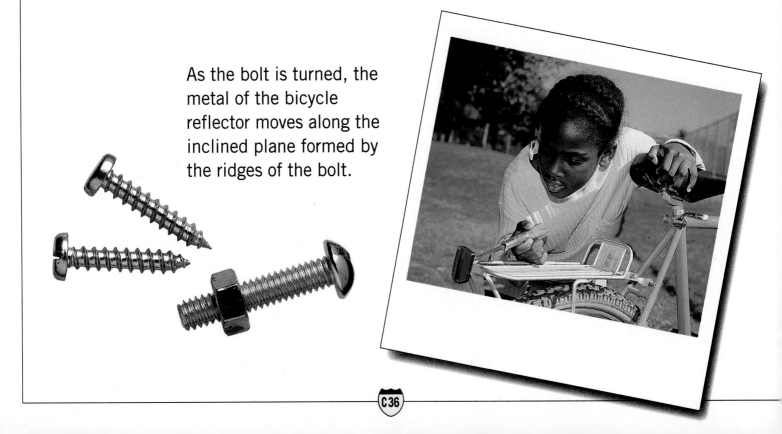

Here are people using chisels, a kind of wedge, to carve wood. Artists start with a square block of wood and create different shapes with a chisel. Where do you think this carved horse will be used?

As you can see, a wedge is made up of two inclined planes. The cutting part of a wedge can be very sharp. This simple machine must be used with great care!

How are you doing?

1. How does an inclined plane make work easier?
2. Give two examples of inclined planes you might find at home.
3. Think What are some ways you might use a wedge?

How do machines that turn help people use forces?

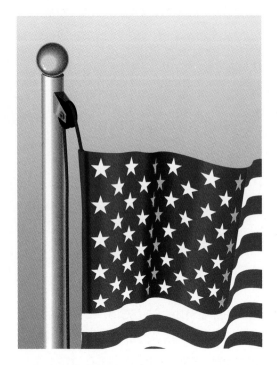

A single pulley attached to the top of a flagpole is used to help raise a flag.

When the bicycle shop opens each morning, the first thing workers do is raise a flag. If you are at the shop when it opens, the workers let you raise the flag.

A **pulley** is a simple machine made of a rope or chain wrapped around a wheel. In raising the flag, you use a single pulley attached to the top of the pole. The pulley changes the direction of your force. You pull down on the rope, and the flag goes up.

Sets of pulley wheels can be used to lift or move heavy weights. Look at the kids pulling on the broomsticks. Two brooms can be used to make a homemade set of pulleys. The broomstick acts like a pulley wheel at each spot where the rope wraps.

Be a Scientist

Can you pull together?

1. Have two classmates each hold a broom as shown in the picture. They should be about 50 cm apart. Tie a rope to the middle of one broom. Loop the rope once over the other broom. Stand next to the person holding the broom to which the rope is tied.

2.  Your classmates will try to keep the brooms apart. You try to move them together by pulling with a steady force on the loose end of the rope. In your Activity Journal, describe what happens.

⚠ Be sure everyone is ready before you start pulling on the rope.

3. Now loop the rope around the brooms several times in a zigzag pattern. Repeat step 2. What happens this time?

What is a wheel and axle?

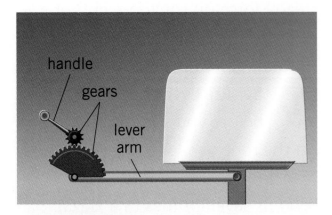

Imagine trying to steer a bicycle that did not have handlebars. Could you control it by trying to grip the little post that the handlebars attach to? Probably not. Your fingers couldn't apply enough force on the post.

The handlebars and post are an example of a simple machine called a wheel and axle. A **wheel and axle** is a machine made of a large wheel attached to a post, or axle.

How does a car window go up and down? Turn the handle and you turn a small gear. That gear turns another bigger gear. A lever connected to this gear moves the window up or down.

The handlebars are a wheel that makes a circle when you turn it. The wheel turns the small post, which is the axle.

Some wheel and axle machines contain gears. A **gear** is a wheel with teeth on its outer edge. When you apply force to the pedals of a bicycle, the pedals turn a large gear called a sprocket. The bicycle chain passes the force to a smaller gear at the rear wheel. That gear is attached to an axle that makes the rear wheel of the bike turn. Many bicycles have several sets of gears. Cyclists shift gears to move uphill and downhill more easily.

The handlebars are attached to a post or axle. The handlebars turn the axle and the axle turns the bicycle's front wheel.

How are you doing?

1. What kind of simple machine would help you to raise the sail on a boat?
2. What does a bike chain do?
3. Think A doorknob is a kind of simple machine. What kind of machine do you think it is? Explain how a doorknob makes work easier.

Maurice's Room

by Paula Fox

Maurice loves to collect things. And that means his room is a mess! These are just a few of the things you'd find there.

There were things with which to make other things, such as nails of different sizes, screws, wire, butterfly bolts, scraps of wood, sockets, filaments from electric-light bulbs, cardboard from grocery boxes, two orange crates, a handsaw and a hammer. On the top of a chest of drawers Maurice kept stones and pebbles, dried tar balls, fragments of brick, pieces of colored bottle glass that had been worn smooth, and gray rocks that glistened with mica. . . .

In another bowl on a table covered with yellow oilcloth were four painted turtles . . . , and in a corner, in a square fish bowl with a chicken-wire roof, lived a garter snake and a lizard.

An old hamster in his cage slept or filled his pouches with dried carrots or ran on his wheel. The wheel, which needed an oiling, screeched all night, the time the hamster preferred for exercise. But the noise didn't keep Maurice awake, only his parents . . .

On the floor were coffee cans with things in them; an eggbeater with a missing gear, a pile of dead starfish, cigar boxes, clockworks, hinges, and a very large grater with sharp dents on all four of its sides. The grater was orange with rust, and it stood in the middle of the room beneath the (dried) octopus. You would have to use a magnifying glass to see all the other things Maurice had found.

Think About Your Reading

1. Write four words that sum up what Maurice's room is like.
2. What kinds of things does Maurice like to collect? List them in three or four categories.

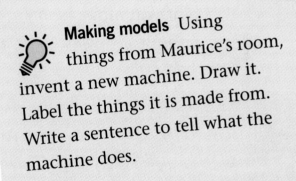

Making models Using things from Maurice's room, invent a new machine. Draw it. Label the things it is made from. Write a sentence to tell what the machine does.

Where to Read More

Ann Cameron, *Julian's Glorious Summer* (Random House, 1987) Find out why Julian hates bicycles —the pedals, tires, wheels, handlebars, and everything!

Looking Back

Words and Concepts

Complete the following statements.

1. A simple machine that changes the direction of the force you apply is called a ____.
2. A wheel and ____ work together to help you turn an object.
3. A ____ helps you move heavy objects without lifting straight up.
4. A simple machine that helps you pry objects apart is a ____.
5. The fixed point on a lever is a ____.
6. Two inclined planes back-to-back make up a ____.
7. Part of the lever that pivots or moves on the fulcrum is the ____.

Applied Thinking Skills

Answer the following questions. You can use words, drawings, and diagrams in your answers.

8. Draw a picture of a can and screwdriver like the one you see. Show the fulcrum and lever arm. How does the lever make work easier?
9. Draw a picture of the screw and the screwdriver like the one you see. Show the wheel and axle.
10. Your World Suppose you wanted to remove a heavy boulder that is half buried in the ground and get it into a truck. What simple machines would you use, and how would you use them?

Show What You Know

When should you use a simple machine?

Observe and Collect Data

1. Try to divide a piece of cloth into three even pieces using only your hands.
2. Use a pair of scissors to cut the cloth.
3. Using your fingers, pick up seeds one at a time and put them in a container.
4. Repeat step 3 using tweezers.

Draw Conclusions

1. Was it easier to divide the cloth with your hands or with the scissors? Explain.
2. Did it take more time to pick up the seeds with your fingers or with tweezers? Explain.

Process Skills

Observing, Inferring

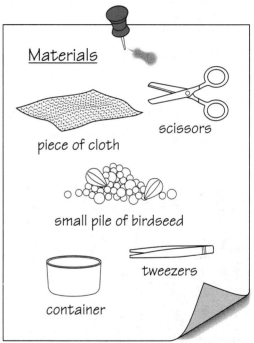

Materials

piece of cloth

scissors

small pile of birdseed

container

tweezers

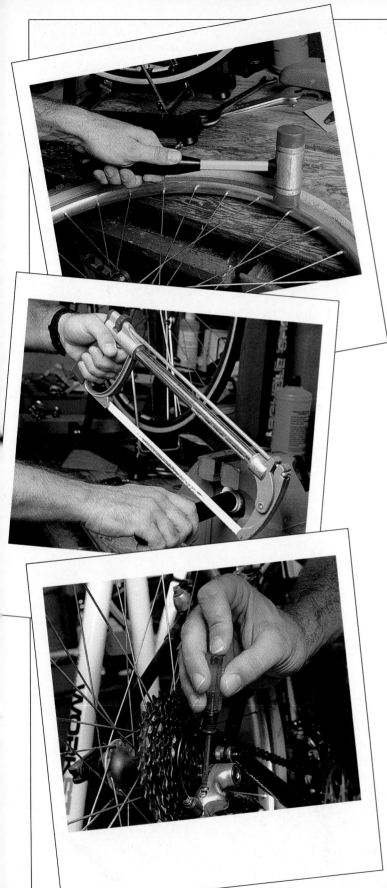

Chapter 3

Compound Machines

In the bike shop, workers use hacksaws, hammers or mallets, bolts, and screwdrivers. They use hammers or mallets to straighten out wheel rims. They use hacksaws to shorten bike seats and handlebars. Look at the bottom photo on this page. The worker is using a small screwdriver to fix a part that helps the bike rider change gears. You can find many interesting tools, or simple machines, inside a bike shop.

Next door to the bicycle shop, a new store is being built. The steel beams for the building are too heavy for people to lift into place. Instead, the workers use a machine called a crane. The crane is a machine that is made up of several simple machines. In your Science Journal, list all of the simple machines you see in the pictures on both pages.

Explore Activity

How can you design a gadget?

HANDS-ON ACTIVITY

Process Skills

Classifying, Making models, Hypothesizing

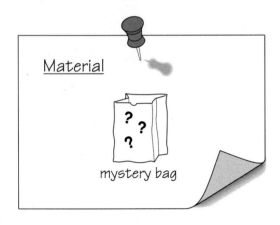

Material

mystery bag

Observe and Collect Data

1. Open the bag your teacher gives you and place the materials on the table. Look over the materials.

2.  Brainstorm a gadget made of simple machines that you could make from your materials. In your Activity Journal, tell what the gadget will be able to do.

3. Make a drawing in your Activity Journal.

4. Build the gadget you designed. Test it to see if it will work.

Share Your Results

Exchange gadgets with another group. How are your gadgets alike? How are they different?

Draw Conclusions

1. What simple machines are in your gadget?
2. Does the machine do anything? Explain.
3. What tasks, if any, can your new invention carry out?

Apply What You Know

1. If your gadget didn't do what you wanted it to, how could you fix it? Did you find that your invention could do something you weren't expecting? Explain.
2. How could you change your gadget so that it could do other tasks?

What is a compound machine?

Recall some of the simple machines you saw at the bike shop. For example, you saw a mallet, a bolt, a gear, and a wheel on a flagpole. What kind of simple machine is each of these? Maybe you saw a machine at the shop that was made of two or more simple machines. Such a machine is called a **compound machine.**

A bicycle is a compound machine. You can see in the drawing on the next page how the different parts of a bicycle are made up of simple machines. This drawing has been done by an engineer. An engineer wants to see how every piece of a bike is going to fit together before he or she builds it. Not all bicycles are designed like the one on the next page. Look at the drawing carefully. If you were creating a bike, what would it look like?

What are some compound machines you might find at school?

If you take off the cover of the pencil sharpener you will see a compound machine. You can see a few gears. The blades of the sharpener are wedges. What kind of simple machine is the handle? Where do you apply force to make the machine sharpen pencils?

Be a Scientist

MINDS-ON ACTIVITY

Can you find compound machines?

Look around the classroom or outside for compound machines. In your Activity Journal, list what you see. Try to identify the simple machines in each compound machine. Draw what you see.

1. The handlebars are part of a wheel and axle used to steer the bike. You could not go around a corner without using this simple machine.

2. The hand brakes are levers that move a force to the tires of a bike to slow or stop it. What is the force used to slow or stop a moving bike?

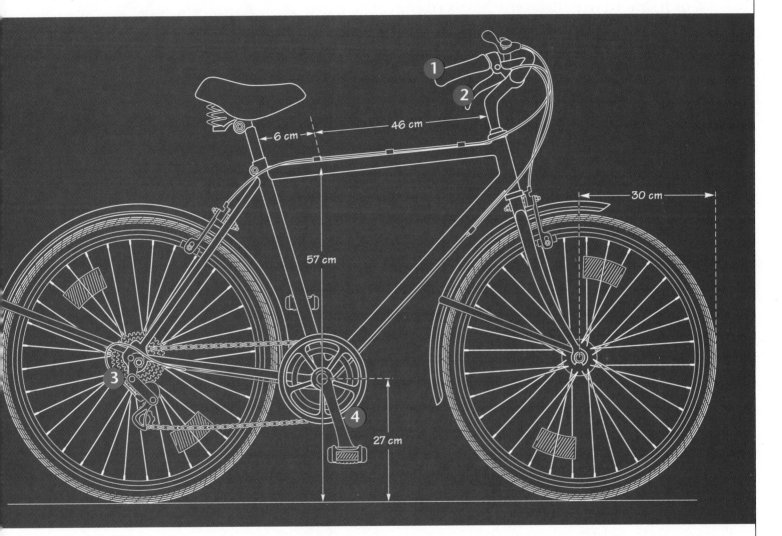

3. The chain moves the force from the sprocket gears to gears on the rear wheel. The rear wheel gears change the number of times the rear wheel turns as the rider moves the pedal gears one complete turn.

4. The pedals are attached to a wheel and axle. The wheel and axle is attached to a gear. The force from the rider's feet and legs move the pedals, wheel and axle, and gear around all at once!

How can you be safe on a bike?

There are many different kinds of bicycles. There are one-speed bikes and five-speed bikes and fifteen-speed bikes. There are dirt bikes and racing bikes and bicycles built for two. And they all make the job of going from one place to another easier, faster, and more fun!

To be safe on a bike, you need to know how to ride it. Before getting on a bike, check to see if everything is working properly. Look at the chain. Is it loose? Never ride a bike that is too big or too small for you. Practice riding in a safe place with someone before riding on the street. Watch out for cars when riding your bike!

When riding a bike, you should always obey the street signs you see. These signs or lights are made to keep everyone near roads safe. You share the road with bikes, cars, people, and other things.

Be a Scientist

Where does the force go?

When you are pedaling a bicycle, you supply all the force. The part of the bike that you supply force to sends the force to other parts of the bike. For example, what happens when you push on the brakes?

Think about some forces you apply to your bicycle. In your Activity Journal, list the different things that happen to that force as it is sent to different parts of the bicycle.

A bicycle helmet is a special kind of tool. When the helmet is hit, the material inside the helmet spreads out the force of the blow. This spreading out of the force can protect your head. You should always wear a helmet when riding a bike.

How are you doing?

1. Name some of the simple machines that are found on a bicycle.
2. Is a lawn mower a compound machine? Explain.
3. Think How does a bicycle brake let you stop?

What compound machines can you find at home?

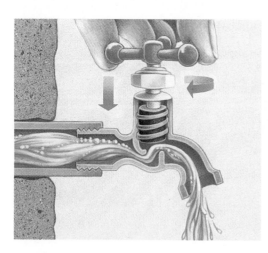

▲ Every time you need water in your home, you must use a compound machine to get it.

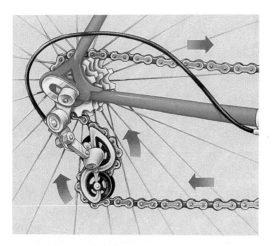

▲ With the flip of a lever, you can change sprockets. This will help you go up and down hills more easily.

You know about one kind of compound machine—a bicycle. You use this machine outdoors on streets, sidewalks, roads, and trails. What are some other compound machines that are used in your home or yard?

Many of the compound machines in your home are powered by motors or engines. Mixers, grinders, and fans are compound machines. Power tools and lawn mowers and cars are also compound machines. In fact, the motors and engines that power these machines are themselves compound machines.

Many of the compound machines in your home are powered by people. Hand mixers, can openers, and pencil sharpeners are compound machines that can be powered by people. Water faucets are compound machines. So, too, are the locks on your doors with the keys that work the locks.

Here is a bike that you might see near your home. Notice that the bike is chained to a fence. Which part of the chain is a compound machine?

![DILEMMA]

How Ramps Are Added to Buildings

When you cross a street, do you notice how high the curb is? What do you think it is like to ride in a wheelchair and come to a step? A small step can block the path of a person who uses a wheelchair.

You may have been in a building that has ramps for wheelchairs. How can you figure out where to place the ramps? Walk around your school and look for places that have ramps. Also look for places that you think should have ramps.

Think About It If you find a place that does not have a ramp, decide if a ramp could be added. If there is no room for a ramp, is there another way a person who uses a wheelchair could go? Draw or write a description about one of these places that needs a ramp.

What are some other compound machines?

Think of the simple machines that can help you use forces to make your work easier: levers, inclined planes, screws, wedges, pulleys, gears, and wheels and axles. Look at the pictures on this page. Before you read more of this page, see if you can figure out how this can opener works. Do you think the person who invented sealed cans also invented the can opener?

The sharp edge of the can opener is a wedge. The handles work as a lever. A wheel and axle moves the blade, or wedge, around the lid of the can you are opening. What does each gear do? They send the force you apply from the wheel and axle to the can.

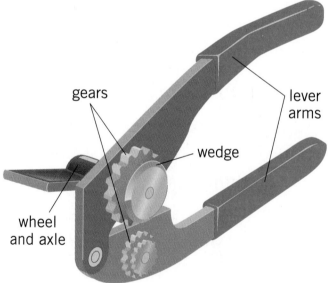

gears

lever arms

wedge

wheel and axle

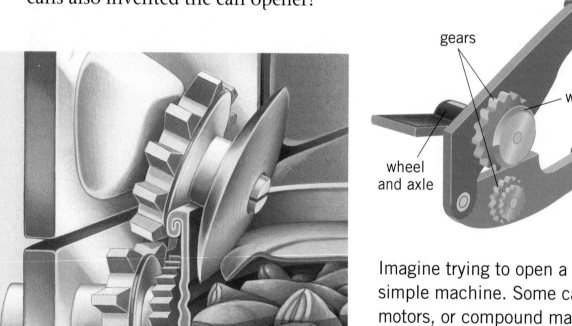

Imagine trying to open a can without a simple machine. Some can openers have motors, or compound machines, attached to them. Which simple machine pictured above could be replaced by a motor?

Rehabilitation Engineer

Being a rehabilitation engineer (rē′hə bil′ə tā′shən en′jə nir′) is very exciting. Hi, my name is Peter Axelson and I am a rehabilitation engineer. A rehabilitation engineer plans and makes machines for people who have special needs. I work all over the United States with people who have special needs.

I have created a hand-powered bike, sit skis, and special wheelchairs. I work with many colleges all over the country. I help students plan and make machines at those colleges. I studied math and engineering in college. And I really like what I do!

How are you doing?

1. Name three compound machines at home that are powered by hand.
2. Explain why a tape dispenser is a compound machine.
3. Think Design a compound machine made up of three simple machines. What does it do?

Looking Back

Words and Concepts

Match the simple machine in Column A with the example in Column B.

Column A	Column B
1. Lever	**a.** Handlebars
2. Inclined plane	**b.** Ax
3. Wedge	**c.** Tire iron
4. Screw	**d.** Flagpole
5. Pulley	**e.** Drill bit
6. Wheel and axle	**f.** Ramp

Applied Thinking Skills

Answer the following questions. You can use words, drawings, or diagrams in your answers.

7. Think of two simple machines and two compound machines. List them as shown below.

Simple Machines

a.

b.

Compound Machines

a.

b.

8. Identify the two simple machines that make a hole punch.

9. Explain why a bike is a compound machine.

10. Your World Make a drawing of a bike. Label three simple machines on your drawing.

Show What You Know

What is in a compound machine?

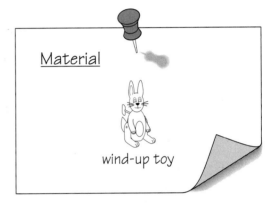

Observe and Collect Data

1. Carefully study the object your teacher gives you.
2. Decide if it is a simple machine or a compound machine.

Process Skills
Observing, Collecting data

Material

wind-up toy

Draw Conclusions

 In your Activity Journal, name the simple machines your object is made of and tell what each does.

Forces & Machines

Show what you know about machines and how they help people use forces. Work by yourself, with a partner, or in a group. Choose one activity.

Mechanical Writer Choose a machine from home to bring to school. Be sure to get an adult's permission. Hide the machine in a box. Write about the machine. Can your classmates figure out what machine is in the box?

Mechanic Invent and construct a compound machine that would help make a job easier. Use at least four simple machines in your invention. Explain and demonstrate your machine.

Car Designer Find a way to make a toy car go faster or farther down an inclined plane. Explain and demonstrate to the class how you improved the toy car.

Songwriter Present a song or jingle to your class on how to sell a bike at a bike shop. Be sure to include how forces make the bike move.

Mechanical Dancer Where on your body can you find simple machines? Move these machines to music. Demonstrate and explain to others how each "body machine" works.

Survival Expert Imagine you are stranded on an island. How might you build a shelter or bring fresh water to you? Describe the machines you need and how you use them. Present your ideas to the class.

Glossary

compound machine (käm pound′ mə shēn′)   A machine made up of two or more simple machines. (page C50)

force (fôrs)   A push or pull. (page C10)

friction (frik′shən)   A force that slows or stops moving objects. (page C14)

fulcrum (ful′krem)   The point that a lever turns on. (page C28)

gear (gēr)   A wheel with teeth on its outer edge. (page C41)

gravity (grav′i tē)   A pulling force between one object and another. (page C12)

inclined plane (in klīnd′ plān)   A kind of simple machine that has a slanted surface. (page C34)

lever (lev′ər)   A simple machine made of an arm or arms that turn on a fulcrum. (page C28)

pulley (pool′ē)   A simple machine made of a rope or chain wrapped around a wheel. (page C38)

screw (skroo)   An inclined plane wrapped around a post. (page C36)

simple machine (sim′pəl mə shēn′)   Something people use to make work easier. (page C28)

wedge (wej)   Two inclined planes joined back-to-back. (page C36)

wheel and axle (hwēl and ak′səl)   A simple machine made of a large wheel attached to a post, or axle. (page C40)

work (werk)   The result of a force making an object move. (page C16)

Unit C Index

Boldface numerals denote glossary terms. Italic numerals denote illustrations.

A

Activities, by name
  Be a Scientist, C14, C18, C29, C35, C39, C50, C52
  Data Collection and Analysis, C21
  Explore, C8–C9, C26–C27, C48–C49
  Show What You Know, C23, C45, C59
Activities, by subject
  compound machines, finding, C50
  compound machines, studying, C59
  force in bicycling, observing, C52
  force on objects, observing, C8–C9
  friction, observing, C14
  gadgets, designing, C48–C49
  inclined plane, using, C35
  lotions and oils, analyzing, C21
  machines, using, C26–C27
  pulling objects, observing, C39
  simple machines, using, C45
  simple machines, using for work, C29
  sliding objects, observing, C23
  work, performing, C18
Arthritis, simple machines for, C33
Axle. *See* Wheel and axle.

B

Bicycle chain, C14, C41, *C51, C54*
Bicycle helmet, *C53*
Bicycle pump, C10, C25
Bicycling
  compound machines and, C46, C50, *C51*

force and, C6, *C6–C7, C11, C51,* C53
gears and, C41
inclined plane and, *C35*
simple machines and, C24–C25, *C46,* C46, *C51*
tires and, *C15,* C24–C25
wheel and axle and, *C41,* C41

C

Careers, rehabilitation engineer, C57
Chisels, *C37*
Compound machines, **C50**
  bicycling and, C50, *C51*
  finding, C50
  at home, *C54,* C54, *C55*
  studying, C59
  types of, C50, *C51, C54, C54, C55, C56*

D

Data Collection and Analysis, C21
Dilemma, ramps for wheelchairs, Technology, C55

F

Force, **C10**
  bicycling and, C6, *C6–C7, C11,* C52
  friction and, C14, *C15*
  gravity and, C12
  objects and, C8–C9, *C19*
  types of, *C10,* C10
  work and, C18, *C19*
Fox, Paula, C42–C43
Friction, **C14,** *C15*
Fulcrum, **C28,** *C28, C30, C31,* C31, *C32,* C32

G

Gadgets, designing, C48–C49
Gear, *C40,* **C41,** *C54*
Gravity, **C12**

I

Inclined plane, **C34**–C35, *C34, C35, C37*

J

Joints
  arthritis and, C33
  as levers, *C32,* C32

L

Levers, **C28,** *C28, C30, C30–C32, C31*
Lifting, *C16*
Lotions, analyzing, C21

M

Machines. *See also* Compound machines; Simple machines.
  friction and, C14
  rehabilitation engineer, C57
  using, C26–C27
  work and, C17
Math Connection, rating lotions and oils, C21
Maurice's Room, C42–C43

O

Oils, analyzing, C21

P

Process skills
  classifying, C48–C49
  collecting data, C59
  hypothesizing, C48–C49
  inferring, C8–C9, C23, C26–C27, C45
  making models, C48–C49
  observing, C8–C9, C23, C26–C27, C45, C59
Pulley, **C38,** *C38*

R

Rehabilitation engineer, C57

S

Science & Literature Connection
  Maurice's Room, C42–C43
Science, Technology & Society
  arthritis, Technology, C33
Screw, **C36,** *C36*
Simple machines, **C28**
  arthritis and, C33
  bicycling and, C24–C25, *C51*
  fulcrum and, *C28,* C28, *C30, C31*
  inclined plane and, *C34, C34–C35, C35, C37*
  levers and, *C28,* C28, *C30–C32,* C30–C32
  pulley, *C38,* C38
  screw, *C36,* C36
  types of, C24–C25
  using, C26–C27, C45
  wedge, C36, *C37*
  wheel and axle, C40–C41
  work and, C29
Sliding objects, C23

T

Tools, C24–C25, C54. *See also* Simple machines.

V

Viewpoint, bicycling as exercise, C20

W

Wedge, **C36,** *C37*
Wheel and axle, **C40**–C41, *C41*
Work, **C16**
  force and, C18, *C19*
  machines and, C17
  simple machines and, C29
  types of, C16, *C17*

Y

You Can Help, C17, C30

Credits

Photographs

4C Bill Everitt/Tom Stack & Associates; 7T Bill Everitt/Tom Stack & Associates; 11B David Madison; 13 Kevin Horan; 18 Michael Austin/Photo Researchers; 20B Alon Reininger/Contact Press Images/Woodfin Camp & Associates; 20TR Thaine Manske/The Stock Market; 24(inset) Matthew McVay/Allstock; 25(inset) David Madison/DUOMO; 35 Gerarg Vandystadt/Agence Vandystadt/Allsport; 37 Jeff Greenberg/Photo Researchers; 47 Richard Pasley/Stock, Boston; 47(inset) Greg Vaughn/Tom Stack & Associates; 52 C. Bruce Forster/AllStock

GHP Studio*   1, 2–3, 24, 25
Ken Karp*   4L, 4R, 5–6, 7B, 10, 11T, 12, 17L, 20TC, 28–31, 36L, 38–39, 40, 44, 53–55, 58

Peter Fox*   19
Tim Davis*   9T, 15, 16, 17R, 22–23, 27, 33–34, 36R, 39, 41, 45–46,`49, 57, 59

Special thanks to Wheelsmith, Palo Alto, California

*Photographed expressly for Addison-Wesley Publishing Company

Illustrations

Nea Bisek   8T, 21, 23, 26T, 45, 48T, 59
Randy Chewning   42–43
Shelton Leong   60–61
Jane McCreary   8B, 13, 26B, 48B
Precision Graphics 14–15, 37, 38, 40, 41, 51, 56R
Margo Stahl   15L, 30, 31, 32, 53, 54, 56L

Text

32 DiSpezio et al., *Science Insights: Exploring Living Thin* (Menlo Park, CA: Addison–Wesley, 1994.) Copyright © Addison–Wesley Publishing Co.

42–43 Paula Fox, *Maurice's Room.* (New York: Macmill Copyright © 1966 by Paula Fox. Edited with the permiss Macmillan Publishing Company.